CELEBRATING EASTER

BY TRUDI STRAIN TRUEIT · ILLUSTRATED BY BENREI HUANG

The Child's World®
childsworld.com

Published by The Child's World®
1980 Lookout Drive • Mankato, MN 56003-1705
800-599-READ • www.childsworld.com

ISBN 9781503853935 (Reinforced Library Binding)
ISBN 9781503854642 (Portable Document Format)
ISBN 9781503855021 (Online Multi-user eBook)
LCCN: 2021930129

Printed in the United States of America

ABOUT THE AUTHOR

Trudi Strain Trueit is a former television news reporter and anchor. She has written dozens of books for children. She lives in Everett, WA with her husband, Bill, a teacher.

ABOUT THE ILLUSTRATOR

Benrei Huang was born and raised in Taiwan and came to live in the United States in 1986. She has illustrated more than twenty-five books for children.

CONTENTS

CHAPTER 1

Happy Easter!

Children race across the grass. They peer into bushes. They peek between **daffodils**. What are they hunting for? Eggs! Today is Easter.

Easter is one of the most important **Christian** holidays of the year. It is when Christians remember the **miracle** of Jesus Christ rising from the dead.

Easter falls on a Sunday between March 22nd and April 25th. In some countries, it may be celebrated in May. The date changes each year, but the holiday always happens in springtime. Why? Flowers bloom in the spring. Animals are born in the spring. The world is waking up after a long winter. Easter is a time to celebrate life!

Spring bursts to-day,
For Christ is risen and
all the earth's at play.
—Christina Rosetti (1830-1894)

Join the fun of an Easter egg hunt!

While there's life, there's hope!
—Roman proverb

5

CHAPTER 2
He Has Risen!

The Easter story is told in the New Testament of the Bible, the Christian book of worship. Christians believe Jesus Christ was God's son.

Jesus lived more than two thousand years ago. He gave **sermons** about how to love God and other people. Jesus performed miracles, such as healing the sick. He had many followers.

Roman leaders worried that Jesus was becoming too powerful. They put him to death on a cross. Jesus was buried in a **tomb**. According to the Bible, three days later, Jesus came back to life! Christians call this the Resurrection, which means to rise from the dead.

> But the angel said to the women, "Do not be afraid, for I know that you seek Jesus who was crucified. He is not here; for he has risen, as he said."
> —The Bible, Matthew 28:5

The Colors of Easter
Purple stands for Christ's death on the cross. White stands for Christ's Resurrection. Gold stands for Christ as "the light of the world."

Jesus Christ had many followers. Easter celebrates Jesus' Resurrection.

CHAPTER 3
A Holy Time

The week before Easter is Holy Week, beginning with Palm Sunday. It is when Christians think about the events that led to the Resurrection. Holy Week begins with remembering Jesus' arrival in Jerusalem. Cheering crowds greeted him waving palm branches. Holy Week ends the following Saturday with Jesus in the tomb.

Many Christian churches hold services during Holy Week. People light candles, sing hymns, and say prayers. In some countries, like Mexico, people march in parades. Thousands may come to watch actors **reenact** Jesus' last days and death.

The Days of Holy Week

Palm Sunday remembers Christ entering Jerusalem.

Maundy Thursday remembers Christ's Last Supper.

Good Friday remembers Christ's death on the cross.

Holy Saturday remembers Christ in the grave.

Many churches have Easter plays.

Sunrise services are attended on Easter Sunday.

People often attend church on Easter Sunday. Religious leaders speak about the meaning of the Resurrection. Christians believe Jesus died for their sins and they will join him one day in heaven. Some churches hold sunrise services outdoors. As the sun comes up, it is a wonderful reminder of the Resurrection.

No one is sure how Easter got its name. Some say it's from the German word *eostarun*, which means "dawn" and refers to the Resurrection. Others say the name is taken from an ancient spring festival called *Eostre* or *Eastre*.

CHAPTER 4
Easter Egg-citement

Bunnies, chicks, and lambs are all **symbols** of Easter. Why? Because they are born in the springtime. Can you think of another Easter symbol of birth? If you answered eggs, you're right!

In **ancient** times, people gave eggs as gifts in the spring. Sometimes, they wrapped their eggs in ferns or flowers and boiled them. This imprinted the pattern of the plant onto the egg. Christians painted their eggs red to symbolize Christ's death. In early America, children colored eggs using dyes made from berries and leaves.

Long ago, people in Eastern Europe made beautiful Easter eggs using beeswax and dye. The eggs were called *pysanky* (peh-SAHN-kee). On Easter morning, everyone got pysanky, even the animals!

Eggs are a symbol of springtime and birth.

Some of the most spectacular eggs in the world came from Russia. In 1885, Peter Carl Fabergé (fah-ber-ZHAY) created a special Easter egg for the queen. The yolk was made of gold. Inside the yolk was a golden hen. Inside the hen was a ruby egg! For many years, Fabergé created dazzling Easter eggs for the Russian royal family.

Did you know Easter has its own flower? It's the Easter lily. The white, trumpet-shaped petals stand for proclaiming the good news of the Resurrection to the world.

CHAPTER 5

Let the Good Times Roll

In the United States, the Easter Bunny hides eggs for children to find on Easter morning. In Germany, children build small nests out of twigs and straw. The Easter Hare hides eggs in the nest during the night. Games are also an Easter **tradition**.

Egg rolling is a popular game that began in Europe hundreds of years ago. The idea is to nudge your egg down a hill using only a spoon. The winner is the one who crosses the finish line first without breaking the egg.

Every year, the President of the United States invites thousands of children to an egg roll at the White House. The winner might get an egg signed by the President!

In Greece, Christians carry an egg with them on Easter Sunday. When friends meet, they tap their eggs together and say, "Christ is risen!"

Egg rolls are a *fun* Easter tradition.

Holiday parades are great fun, too. New York City has held an Easter parade since the 1850s. People wear silly costumes and fancy bonnets, or hats. They march down Fifth Avenue. Anyone can join in the parade.

It's the custom in Germany to gather up everyone's Christmas trees on Easter. The old trees are tossed onto a big bonfire. The Easter Fire marks the end of winter and the beginning of spring.

CHAPTER 6
Foods of the Season

It is no wonder people love to eat at Easter. After all, food **nourishes** life! Breads and cakes are typical Easter foods.

In England, hot cross buns are usually eaten on Good Friday. A cross made of white icing tops each sweet bun. It is a symbol of Christ on the cross. People in Greece make an Easter bread called *tsoureki* (tsoo-REH-kee). Several eggs that have been dyed red are baked right into the ring of dough! In Russia, a fruit and nut bread called *kulich* (KOO-leech) is baked in a coffee can so it will stand very tall. The bread is eaten with a creamy cheese dish called *paskha* (PAHS-kah).

Good Friday comes this month, the old woman runs, with one or two a penny hot cross buns.
—*Poor Robin's Almanack, 1733*

Families may also share an Easter meal. In the United States, it is tradition to serve ham and potatoes. In Sweden, people eat fish, lamb, and boiled eggs. Do you have a favorite Easter food?

CHAPTER 7

Poetry Corner

EASTER BELLS

I think of the garden after the rain;
And hope to my heart comes singing,
"At morn the cherry-blooms will be white,
And the Easter bells be ringing!"

—Edna Dean Procter (1829–1923)

'Twas Easter-Sunday. The full-blossomed trees Filled all the air with fragrance and with joy.

—Henry Wadsworth Longfellow (1807–1882)

EASTER PRAYER FOR CHILDREN

Time for joy and time for giving
Time for remembering
Love while living.

Take this message Easter Day
Show kindness, care
At home and play.

It's in our very acts of giving
Easter's joy
Makes life worth living.

Children round the globe now hear
Keep Easter
In your heart all year.

May joy and love spread land to land
Linked heart to heart
And hand to hand!

—Susan Kramer, author

CHAPTER 8

Songs of Easter

JESUS CHRIST IS RISEN TODAY

Jesus Christ is risen today, Alleluia!

Our triumphant holy day, Alleluia!

Who did once upon the cross, Alleluia!

Suffer to redeem our loss. Alleluia!

—words by Charles Wesley (1707-1788)

THE WORLD ITSELF KEEPS EASTER DAY

The world itself keeps Easter Day,
And Easter larks are singing;
And Easter flowers are blooming,
And Easter buds are springing.
Alleluia! Alleluia!
The Lord of all things lives anew,
And all His works are living too.
Alleluia, alleluia.

—*John Mason Neale (1818–1866)*

Earth's saddest day
and gladdest day were
just three days apart!
—*Susan Coolidge (1835–1905)*

FIVE LITTLE EASTER EGGS

Five little Easter eggs, lovely colors wore;
Mother ate the blue one, then there were four.
Four little Easter eggs, two and two, you see;
Daddy ate the red one, then there were three.
Three little Easter eggs, before I knew;
Sister ate the yellow one, then there were two.
Two little Easter eggs, oh, what fun;
Brother ate the purple one, then there was one.
One little Easter egg, see me run;
I ate the last one, and then there was none!

—*Author Unknown*

The great gift of Easter is hope—Christian hope which makes us have that confidence in God, in his ultimate triumph, and in his goodness and love, which nothing can shake.
—*Basil C. Hume (1923-1999)*

JOINING IN THE SPIRIT OF EASTER

* Are you Christian? If so, talk about the Easter story with your family. What does the Resurrection mean to you?

* Do you know someone from another country? Ask about what he or she does to celebrate Easter.

* Gather your friends and family for an egg roll. All you need are some plastic spoons and a gentle slope to hold the race. (Don't try this on a steep hill!)

* Make an Easter card and give it to someone who has done something nice for you or who may be alone on Easter, like an elderly neighbor.

* Go to an Easter parade, plant flowers, or visit a farm with newborn lambs to celebrate the arrival of spring!

MAKING AN EDIBLE BIRD'S NEST

What you need:

Wax paper
Paper plates
1 bag of crunchy chow-mein noodles
1 bag of chocolate chips
Peanut butter
1 bag of jelly beans
Candy-coated chocolate eggs
Marshmallow chicks

Directions

1. Place squares of wax paper onto eight paper plates (one plate for each nest). Place chow-mein noodles in a large bowl.

2. Pour chocolate chips into a separate bowl that is safe to use in the microwave. Have an adult help you heat the chocolate chips in the microwave until they are melted.

3. Pour the melted chocolate over the chow-mein noodles. Mix the noodles with a spoon until they are completely covered in chocolate.

4. Spoon a small mound of the chocolate noodles onto each plate. Let the mounds cool a bit so you can touch them, but don't wait too long or they will harden.

5. Shape each mound into a nest. Use peanut butter as glue to stick jelly beans and candy-coated chocolate eggs inside the nest. Use more peanut butter to attach a marshmallow chick to the edge of the nest or inside it.

6. Use your bird nests as Easter gifts, decorations, or yummy treats to eat!

MAKING AN EASTER EGGSHELL MOSAIC

What you need:

1 freezer bag filled with pieces
   of colored eggshells from
   your Easter eggs
1 large sheet of poster board
   or heavy paper
1 Pencil
1 Paint brush
Glue

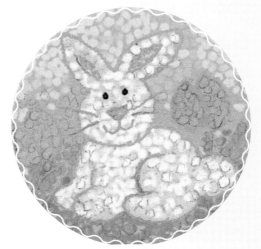

Directions

1. Crush the eggshells while they are in the sealed bag to break up the bigger pieces.

2. Draw the outline of a bunny, chick, or cross on your poster board. You can also make up a design as you go along.

3. Using a paintbrush, dab glue onto a small section of the poster board. Carefully arrange pieces of eggshell onto the glue (with the color-side up).

4. As you work, leave a sliver of space between each shell to let the poster board show through. This will allow you to achieve the mosaic effect.

5. Keep working in small sections across the board, applying glue and attaching eggshells.

6. When you are finished, let your project dry for a few hours.

Your Easter mosaic is now ready to frame, hang on the fridge, or give as a gift!

GLOSSARY

ancient (AYN-shunt)—very old; usually meaning thousands of years

Christian (KRISS-chen)—a person who believes in Jesus Christ and his teachings

daffodils (DAFF-uh-dilz)—bright yellow flowers that bloom in the spring

miracle (MIR-uh-kull)—a wondrous event with no human explanation

nourishes (NUR-ish-ez)—provides things necessary for growth and good health

reenact (ree-en-AKT)—to act out an event that took place in the past

sermons (SUR-munz)—speeches that teach a religious or moral lesson

symbol (SIM-bull)—an object that stands for an idea

tomb (TOOM)—a burial chamber

tradition (truh-DISH-un)—a long-held custom or something people do every year

LEARN MORE

BOOKS

Cosson, M. J. *Easter Traditions around the World.* Mankato, MN: The Child's World, 2022.

Heiligman, Deborah. *Holidays Around the World: Celebrate Easter.* Washington, DC: National Geographic Kids, 2016.

Kolibová, Renata. *Spring and Easter Paper Crafting with Reny.* Czech Republic: 2020.

Miller, Jean. *The Story of Easter.* New York, NY: Golden Books, 2018.

Polacco, Patricia. *Rechenka's Eggs.* New York, NY: Paper Star, 1996.

WEBSITES

Visit our website for links about Easter and other holidays:
childsworld.com/links

Note to Parents, Teachers, and Librarians: We routinely verify our Web links to make sure they are safe and active sites. So encourage your readers to check them out!

INDEX